# My Mother

### Used to Say

Valerie Bowe

summersdale

# Introduction

The idea for this book first came to me when I was reading Brian Keenan's autobiography, *An Evil Cradling*. I remember a scene in the book in which, in order to help John McCarthy to move out of his distress, the author keeps repeating something that John's mother used to say to his father. It left a lasting impression on me. It struck me then how very potent these repetitive sayings we hear in childhood are, and the lasting influence they have on us. The seed was planted.

After that I began to notice that in practically every interview, celebrities would recall what their parents said to them as children. In my work as a coordinator in adult and community education I chatted to a number of the participants and they too remembered what their mother or father or grandparents used to say. I thought about my own parents and, lo and behold, I began to recall vividly what I had heard in childhood. I felt confident, then, that all families have this oral tradition that is succinctly gathered into phrases or sayings. In fact, our parents taught us through this oral wisdom.

I talked about the idea for the book for a good while, really because I wasn't sure how to go about it until a friend told me to stop talking about it and just do it. Oh! How do you do that? Write to people and ask them! It was put up to me – fair and square.

In the evenings I would write a couple of letters. It became a hobby; like my hobby in childhood of collecting words of wisdom in a scrapbook that I had cut out from my mother's towering collection of past editions of the *Woman's Weekly*. I still wasn't fully sure if it would work, but, when Sir Alex Ferguson contributed I knew then that the book was possible.

The book was published and became a bestseller in Ireland and here is a new edition, with new contributions. Let it walk you down memory lane and look back with new interest at the words your mother/father/grandparents uttered to you to guide you through life.

I would like to thank those who so generously contributed to the book, without whom it would have not been possible.

Valerie Bowe

# Notes from the author

While the book is titled *My Mother Used to Say*, contributors were invited to provide sayings handed down by mothers, fathers or grandparents but the majority contributed what their mother used to say.

For readers unfamiliar with the title 'TD', it means Teachta Dála – a member of the Irish Dáil or parliament.

Part of the proceeds of this book will go to the Kitty Whittle Fund which provides education bursaries for lone parents.

My mother always said, 'In life you should always have a really good bed and a really good pair of shoes, because you are either in one or the other.'

Gloria Hunniford, TV presenter and founder of The Caron Keating Foundation

My mother always used to say
'Always be yourself – and always
take a safety pin when you go out.'

Cornelia Frances, actress

My father always used to say, 'Life is full of small beginnings.'

Andrea Corr, musician

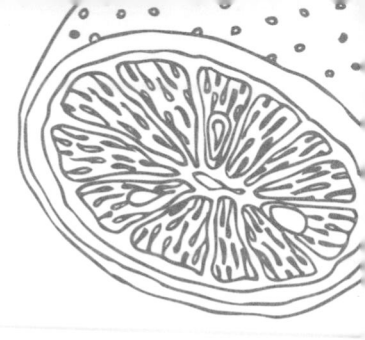

My mother used to say, 'Be a
first-rate version of yourself, not a
second-rate version of someone else.'

Liza Minnelli, actress/singer

My grandmother, Molly Darcy, always used to say, 'Every day you can get out of bed is a great day.'

Bill Cullen, businessman/host of *The Apprentice* (Ireland)

My mother always used to say, 'It takes all sorts to make a world.'

Jeremy Irons, actor

My mother taught me to walk proud and tall 'as if the world was mine.'

Sophie Loren, actress

'Everything comes home,' my mother used to say; every word spoken, every shadow cast, every footprint in the sand. It can't be helped; it's part of what makes us who we are.

Joanne Harris, author

My mother used to say, 'If somebody's not nice to you, be nice to them,' and if I asked why, she'd say, 'To show them you're a nice person,'

*and*

'A tree without roots is just a piece of wood.'

Marco Pierre White, chef

My mother always used to say, 'The mind is like a parachute – it doesn't work unless it's open.'

Sean Barrett, TD, Cean Comhairle, Speaker of the House, Dáil Éireann

*Ma mère a toujours dit, 'Regarde toujours devant, jamais – derrière.'* ('Always look forward, never backwards.')

Pierre Cardin, fashion designer

Mum used to say, 'A new broom sweeps clean, but an old broom knows the corners.'

Ainsley Harriott, chef

My mother used to say, 'The outside world doesn't have a lot to offer, you have to make your own heaven in your own home.'

Bette Midler, singer/actress/comedienne

My mother always used to quote the poet Tagore: 'Nothing lasts forever, brother – nothing lasts for long. Keep that in your heart and rejoice.'

Joanna Lumley, actress

My mother, Mary, used to say, 'Never trouble trouble until trouble troubles you. For if you trouble trouble, trouble will trouble you.'

Fiona Hoban, author/psychotherapist

My mother used to say, 'You judge your contribution by what you have done for the most vulnerable.'

The Hon Wayne Swan, Deputy Prime Minister and Treasurer of Australia

My grandmother's wisest saying, when anyone criticised her method of doing something was, 'Everyone has a way, and every way does.' We all get there in the end.

Lorely Burt, MP for Solihull

My father always used to say, 'Never the backward glance – energy lost on worrying about the past is wasted energy.'

Simon Coveney, TD, Minister for Agriculture, Fisheries and Food, Dáil Éireann

My maternal grandmother, who partly brought me up, told me as a child that I should wish no one ill will, otherwise it could fall on me. I took the point in my adult life.

David Winnick, MP for Walsall North

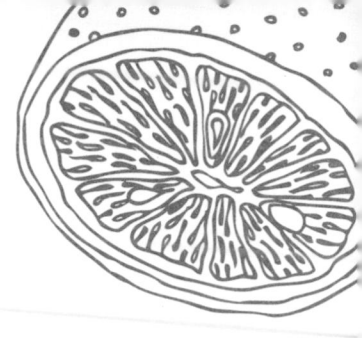

My father's advice to me was,
'You should have three basic
principles to guide you through life:
(a) Be the best in whatever you do,
(b) Be magnanimous, and
(c) Serve the community.'

Lord Sheikh

My mother always used to say,
'Two wrongs are never right.'

Kevin Dundon, hotel owner

My mother always used to say,
'Never be turned by the
flattering tongue,'

*and*

'Imagination keeps the crows flying.'

My father used to say, 'You can take
a horse to the well but a pencil
is always lead.'

Bernard Farrell, playwright

My mother always used to say, 'God never closes one door without opening another.'

Eamonn Gilmore, Tánaiste, Deputy Prime Minister of Ireland

My parents used to say, 'You are judged in life by what you give, not by what you get.'

David Jamilly, entrepreneur

My mother used to say,
'Look before you leap.'

Bernard Jenkin, MP for Harwich
and North Essex

My mother used to say,
'It's no use crying over spilt milk.'

My mother always said,
'No one can judge you apart from
yourself, and that's the one judge
you can't fool,'

*and*

'Blue and green should never be seen
except in the eyes of an Irish colleen.'

Chi Onwurah, MP for Newcastle-upon-Tyne
Central

My mother always used to say,
'Nobody can out-do the Lord
in generosity.'

Niall Quinn, chairman of Sunderland FC

My mother's favourite saying was, 'The road to Hell is paved with good intentions.'

Sir Gerry Robinson, businessman/former head of Granada TV

My father used to say, 'You can never put an old head on young shoulders.' I wondered why you would want to – now I know.

Rt Hon Joan Ruddock, MP for Lewisham Deptford

My mother always used to say,
'Nice is as nice does,'

*and*

'Show me your friends and I'll tell
you what you are.'

Paula Tilbrook, actress

My mother used to say,
'I've seen it all before.'

Enda Kenny, An Taoiseach, Prime Minister of
Ireland

When I left school I decided to go to France as an au pair to learn French. I was waiting for my friend who said she wanted to go too. After a couple of months of waiting my mother asked me when was I going to France. I said I was waiting for my friend. My mother then said, 'If you're always waiting for someone to do something with you, you'll never do anything in life.' My friend wasn't really committed to going and soon after I left for France.

Another of her sayings – she loved style and she would often say, 'Never tell your husband how much you paid for a dress.'

**Valerie Bowe, author**

My mother used to say to me,
'What's for you won't pass you.'

Sorcha Furlong, actress

My Dad always told me,
'Good things come to
those who wait!'

Jamie Roberts, rugby player

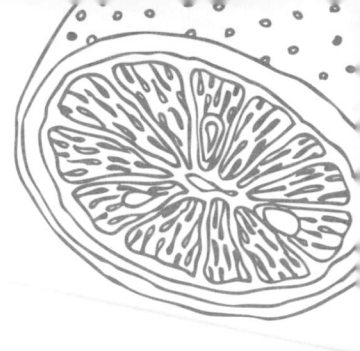

*Ma mère a toujours dit,*
*'Quand on veut, on peut.'*
('When you want to do
something, you can do it.')

Edouard Loubet, chef

My mother used to say,
'As you get older the years pass
much more quickly, don't
wish your life away.'
Now I wish I had listened to her.

Michael McCann, MP for East Kilbride, Strathaven and Lesmahagow

My mother used to say,
'There's none so queer as folk'
as she was from Yorkshire; but she
also said, 'Do the right thing not for
a round of applause but because it is
the right thing to do.'

Nick Knowles, TV presenter

My mother used to say,
'You're as good as anyone but better
than nobody.'

When it came to dividing things
like cake or chocolate bars with my
brother, when we were children, she
always said, 'One cut it in half, and
the other gets first choice.' A perfect
way to make sure that both pieces
were identical!

Stephen Dixon, newsreader

I remember my mother frequently telling me, 'Be careful what you want, for if you really want it hard enough, you might just get it.'

Brian Keenan, writer/broadcaster

My mother used to say,
'Today's thugs, tomorrow's heroes,'

*and*

'Everybody is shy, at least as shy as
you are, remember that.'

Shane McGowan, singer/songwriter

My mother used to say,
'When you look in the mirror of
a morning you have to be happy
with who you see, not embarrassed.
Always make choices for the right
reasons, no matter how hard it is.'

Stephen McPartland, MP for Stevenage

My mother had a lot of sayings that have stuck with me over the years. I think the one, 'Life is for living, not for throwing away' is one that gets more potent the older I get.

Bryan Murray, actor

My mother, Peggy, always used to say, 'You'll have to eat a ton of dirt before you die.'

Sean McMahon, author

My father always used to say, 'If you can be yourself for at least one-third of your life, you'll always win.'

Finbar Furey, singer/songwriter

My mother always used to say,
'Good God, tonight.'

Bertie Ahern, former Taoiseach (former prime
minister of Republic of Ireland)

My mother, Hallfridur O'Neill, used to say, 'What will be, will be.'

Rachel Allen, chef

My mother used to say,
'Fools and bairns shouldn't
see things half done.'

Lord Attlee

My mother always used to say,
'What is seldom is wonderful,'

*and*

'A nod is as good as a wink to
a blind horse.'

Frances Black, singer/songwriter

My mother always used to quote a neighbour of ours, a Scotch woman whose accent she was also very fond of imitating: 'It's no' the things you bargain for, Mrs Heaney, it's the things that crop up.'

Seamus Heaney, poet

My mother used to say,
'You can tell what a man wants
you to think of him by his tie.
You can tell what a man thinks of
himself by his shoes.'

Paddy Ashdown, politician/diplomat

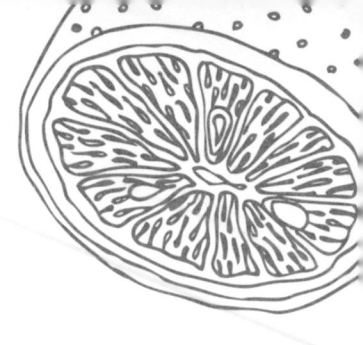

My mother always used to say,
'You'd excite a nation.'

Niall McMonagle, writer/critic

My mother used to say,
'Life is one per cent inspiration
and 99 per cent perspiration,'

*and*

'Before ever passing comment on
someone try to walk a mile
in their shoes.'

Esther McVey, MP for Wirral West

*Ma mère a toujours dit,*
*'Bien faire et laisser braire.'*
('Do your best and don't
mind the critics.')

Brigitte Bardot, actress

When I am giving speeches at prize-giving ceremonies, I always suggest they live their life by my mother's saying, 'Do your best.' If you do your best then you can't let yourself or anyone else down as no one can ask for more.

Dame Anne Begg, MP for Aberdeen South

My father used to say,
'Procrastination is the thief of time.'

Donovan, musician/songwriter

My mother always used to say,
'Dreams are for dreamers, Ronan.
Goals are for you and me.'

Ronan Tynan, doctor/tenor

My mother and father used to say, 'Just give it a go; you never know what can happen.'

Tim Visser, rugby player

My mother used to say,
'The only people that don't make
mistakes are those who
don't do anything.'

Gavin Williamson, MP for South Staffordshire

My mother used to tell me that
despite my humble background,
(I grew up on a council estate)
I was as good as anyone else.
She was right.

Gordon Henderson, MP for Sittingbourne
and Sheppey

My mother used to say,
'Never forget: you're as good as
anyone else and, my word,
don't let anyone make you
believe differently.'

Baroness Tina Stowell

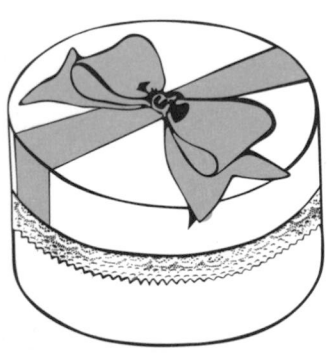

My mother always used to say,
'There is light at the end of the
tunnel.'

Damien Duff, footballer

My mother used to say,
'If everybody put their trouble in
a bundle, and all of them put their
bundles on the floor in the same
room, people would look at
the other bundles and then
pick up their own bundle
and go away.'

Sir Gerald Kaufman, MP for
Manchester Gorton

My mother used to say,
'A peacock that sits on its feathers
is just another turkey.'

Stephen Myler, rugby player

The very best advice my mother ever
gave me was the old Yorkshire expression,
'Spit on yer 'ands an' tek a fresh 'old.'
She sent me these sage words in a letter when
I was going through a bad time at the
Royal Academy of Music in the seventies and
they have come back to help me at
difficult times ever since.
Together with the letter were a
handful of stones, which fell on my feet as
I opened the envelope. There was a further
note explaining what they were.
It read, 'It sounded like you needed some
Yorkshire grit – so I sent you some.
Love Mum.'

Lesley Garrett, soprano

My mother always used to say,
'If you're bored, it's an
insult to yourself.'

Enda O'Coineen, yachtsman/entrepreneur

My mother used to say,
'Don't look backwards, you're
not going in that direction.'

Carol Thatcher, journalist

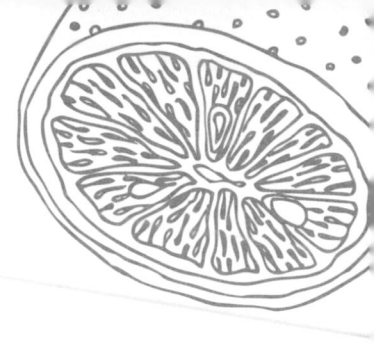

My mother used to say,
'Don't come running to me if
you break your leg.'

Danny Crates, athlete, Paralympic gold medallist

My mother used to say,
'Give someone enough love and they
will give it back.' And whenever I got myself
in a tizz she would say 'Palms Up.' When I had
a horrible time or something awful happened
she would always tell me to go to sleep because
tomorrow was a new day and everything
would look better then. It always did,
even if it was only a little better.

Lynda Bellingham, TV presenter

My mother always used to say,
'Look after your brothers
and sisters.'

Mohamed Al Fayed, businessman

My mother:
'It was she who taught me to
get up every day and keep going;
To look for the best in people even
when they saw the worst in me;
To be grateful for every day
and greet it with a smile;
To believe I could do or be anything
I put my mind to if I was willing
to make the requisite effort;
To believe that, in the end, love and
kindness would prevail over
cruelty and selfishness.'

Bill Clinton, former president of the
United States of America

My father, Ginger O'Brien,
has two sayings I find helpful:
'Every day is a new one,'

*and*

'Walk before you run.'

Kevin O'Brien, cricketer

We spent many wonderful sunny
Sundays on the beaches in Connemara
and this following saying of my father's still
conjures up the excitement and anticipation
of heading off for sing-songs and sandwiches
and lemonade, not knowing which beach we
were going to on any given day. There was
always the element of mystery and surprise
and absolute wonder, as he said,
'All aboard for Oranmore,
Shanghai and Galway.'

**Martina Stanley, actor**

My mother used to say,
'Cheer up for Chatham,
Gravesend's in sight.'

Alan Rusbridger, editor of *The Guardian*

When my twin and I quarrelled
my parents used to say, 'Little birds in
their nest agree.' When they and their friends
were lighting cigarettes my parents used to say,
'Never take the third light,' a superstition from
the Great War in which my father fought. If
I was picking my nose my mother would say,
'Bring us down a picture of the Pope.'

Michael Longley, poet

Mum always used to say,
'I'm just reporting,' when she was
passing on any criticism of me.

Ed Vaizey, MP for Wantage

I write this on what would
have been my mother's 82nd birthday.
She had many sayings
and this one I remember with a
smile: 'You found it before
it was lost.'

Paul Goggins, MP for Wythenshawe and Sale East

When things went wrong my
mother would say, 'Ah well, worse things
happen at sea.' The words of wisdom she gave
me when I had kids of my own were, 'The best
gifts you can give your children are roots and
wings.' She meant, give them the confidence to
leave you and go out into the world,
and the assurance that they can
always come back home.

Alan Cotton, landscape painter

My mother, Susan, was devastated when
her mother, Granny White, died in 1959.
I often found her crying when the song
'A Mother's Love's a Blessing'
came on the radio:
'A mother's love's a blessing,
no matter where you roam.
Keep her while she's living
'cause you'll miss her when she's gone.
Love her as in childhood,
though, feeble, old and grey,
For you'll never miss your mother's love
till she's buried beneath the clay.'

Danny Morrison, author

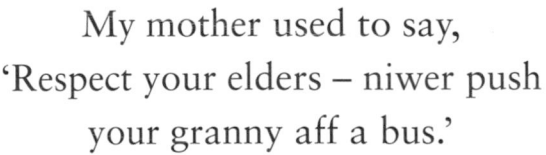

My mother used to say,
'Respect your elders – niwer push
your granny aff a bus.'

Lord Stewart Sutherland of Houndwood

My mother used to say, upon seeing a woman she neither liked nor thought was attractive, 'Darling, she looks like the north end of a horse, facing south.' To this day I still don't know what she meant, but it must be politically incorrect!

The Earl of Shrewsbury and Waterford

My father always used to say,
'Remember your roots and
where you came from.'

Pat Rabbitte, TD, Minister for Communications,
Energy and Natural Resources, Republic of Ireland

I had so many freckles growing up that my mother used to say that they were kisses from the angels.

Lara Flynn Boyle, actress

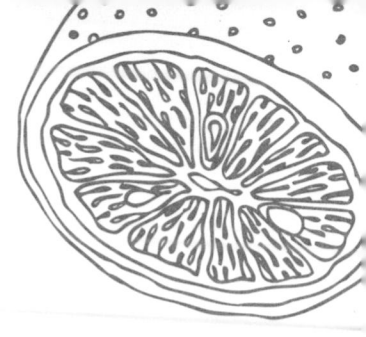

My mother's advice to mothers
of younger children was, 'Keep your
mouth shut and your door open.'
Another one was the recipe for
good family relationships with your
son-in-law and daughter-in-law:
'Don't voice an opinion unless you're
asked for it and don't visit unless
you are invited.'

Darina Allen, chef

My mother always used to say,
'Your mother's never wrong.'

Diarmuid Gavin, garden designer/TV presenter

My mother's family came from
Flanders via Cobh to South Wales.
I remember well two things she used
to say; 'It is not who you become
that matters; just remember
where you come from,'

*and*

'Son, in life you will find that sense
is not that common.'

The Rt Hon Lord Touhig of Islwyn
and of Glansychan

My mother used to say,
'Your face is not your fortune.'

Baroness Deech

My mother always used to say,
'Marry for money and you'll earn it.'

Michael Colgan, film producer/theatre director

My mother used to say,
'A real man doesn't just flirt
with the pretty faces.'

John Mann, MP for Bassetlaw

My grandmother told me,
'Grief is the price we pay for love.'

Prince William, Duke of Cambridge

My mother always used to say,
'It takes two to tango.'

Jennifer Johnston, author

My father used to say,
'Let me give you the advice the
old cat gave to the young kitten:
always purr when you're pleased.'

Lord Robert Armstrong

My mother always used to say,
'Be nice to people on the way up,
they will be waiting for you on
the way down.'

Sharon Osbourne,
businesswoman/*American Idol* judge

My mother would often say, 'Make sure you always adapt to your surroundings.'

Mo Farah, athlete, gold medallist at the World Athletics Championships

My mother used to say,
'Do unto others as you would
be done by.'

Arlene Phillips, choreographer/former *Strictly Come Dancing* judge

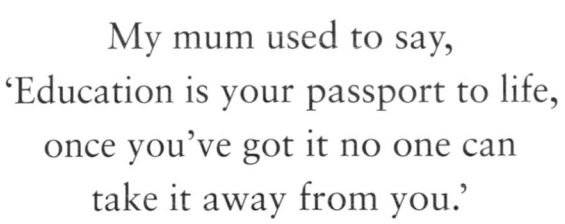

My mum used to say,
'Education is your passport to life,
once you've got it no one can
take it away from you.'

Baroness Floella Benjamin

My mother used to say,
'There's never a convenient time to
have babies.' I've always used that as a
metaphor for starting businesses.

*and*

'Isn't this fun?'
Usually when it wasn't.

*and*

'Let's put all that behind us and think
of something happy.'

**Simon Woodroffe OBE, entrepreneur/founder of
YO! Sushi**

My mother, who was also a
published author, used to say,
'I'm always suspicious of a
house without books,'

*and*

'Take time and care will ensue.'

Finn MacEoin, author

My mother Bernadette always used to give me this good advice: 'Love many, trust few, always paddle your own canoe.'

Patricia Scanlan, author

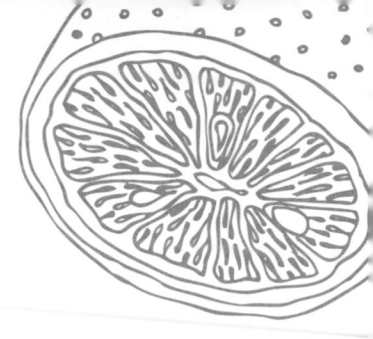

My mother used to say,
'Spend what you have in *your* bank
account, not somebody else's.'

Chris Whitehead, rugby player

My father always used to say, 'People who don't ask how much don't intend to pay.'

Peter Cunningham, author/journalist

My mother always used to say,
'Look after the pennies and
the pounds will look
after themselves.'

Paraic Duffy, Director General of the
Gaelic Athletic Association

My grandma always said,
'If a job's worth doing, it's worth
doing well.' And that's as true
today as it was then.

Cherie Blair, QC

My mother used to say,
'Lazy people take most pains.'

John Redwood, MP for Wokingham

My mother used to say,
'If at first you don't succeed,
try, try and try again.'

Pauline Latham OBE, MP for Mid Derbyshire

My mother, Sybil le Brocquy, used to say, 'Always keep the taxi if you want to arrive at your destination.'

Louis le Brocquy, artist

My mother always used to say, 'Prepare yourself, the opportunity will come.'

Gay Byrne, broadcaster

My mother used to say,
'Remember, it's not who you
know... oh yes it is.'

Toby Booth, head coach for
London Irish Rugby Club

The best advice I've ever been
given was from my grandmother:
'Darling, it's not how you're doing,
it's what you're doing.'

One expression my mother used
a lot was 'They that can't
schemey must louster.'
(Those that can't use their brains
have to use their hands.)

*and*

'He's maize as a brish.'
(Stupid as a brush.)

Stephen Gilbert, MP for St Austell and Newquay

While growing up on a farm in County Meath my mother always told me, 'Keep your principles.' A very valuable lesson, especially in the business world.

Richard Corrigan, chef

My mother used to say,
'Nobody ever moved forward by
patting themselves on the back.'

Andrew Bridgend, MP for North West
Leicestershire

My father always used to say,
'Do anything you want with your
life, but just don't go to sea.'

Dermot Bolger, author/playwright

My father always used to say,
'If I ever see you at the pit gates,
I'll kick your backside all
the way home.'

Sir Michael Parkinson, broadcaster

My mother always used to say,
'Fine food, starch removed,'

*and*

'If you have a talent, never hide it.'

Nick Munier, maître d'

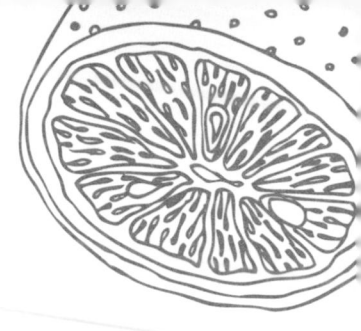

My mother is a great believer in
the healing power of plenty of
sleep, and if there was ever anything
wrong with you she would say,
'Get a big glass of water and some
vitamins into you and get to
bed, and you'll wake up as
right as rain – you'll be
one hundred per cent.'

Tommy Bowe, rugby player

My mother used to say,
'Sitting is bad for your complexion.'

Xenia, model

My mother used to say,
'When you have a headache,
always take a laxative as well
as a painkiller.'

*and*

'In the bath, always wash your
cleanest bits first.'

Lord Skelmersdale

The saying I remember most
from my late father was,
'What you need is more fresh
air and exercise.'

Ann McKetchin, MP for Glasgow North

My father used to say regarding the drinking of alcohol, 'Two is plenty, four is only half enough.'

Kevin Brennan, MP for Cardiff

My mother always used to say,
'Don't let your eyes be bigger than
your stomach.'

Tony Blair, former prime minister
of the United Kingdom

My mother always used to say,
'Listen to your body when eating.'

Pauline Bewick, artist

Mother as I started my dancing lessons: 'When you step on your dance partner's foot never apologise as she is likely to think the event was her fault.'

Father often said, 'Decisions made during or after dinner should always be carefully reconsidered in the morning.'

Peter, Lord Temple-Morris

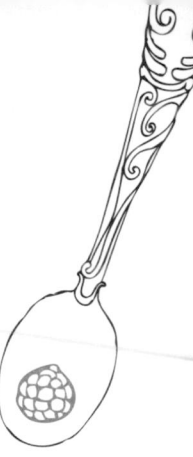

My mother used to say, 'Eat your rice pudding even if it's cold. Lots of children won't get any rice pudding.' (Lucky them, I thought.)

Lord Timothy Renton of Mount Harry

My mother always used to say,
'If you bake in anger, it will taste of
doubt and you will make an
unhappy cake.'

Hugo Hamilton, author

My mother always used to say,
'You can't cook unless you're
in the kitchen.'

Mary Coughlan, former Tánaiste (former deputy
prime minister of Republic of Ireland)

From my mother via her mother,
'Never go into the kitchen
empty-handed.'

Charles Kennedy, MP for Ross, Skye and Lochaber

My mum's best advice to us
all was, 'Be kind.'

John McDonnell, MP for Hayes and Harlington

My mother used to say, 'You'll be laughing on the other side of your face.' This was a fairly frequent reminder from my mother not to get too arrogant or too cocky.

Steve McCabe, MP for Selly Oak, Birmingham

My father's advice to me was,
'Never argue over matters of easily
ascertainable fact.'

Lord Roper

My mother used to say, 'Patience is a virtue rarely seen in a woman and never in a man.'

Ben Ainslie, athlete, Olympic gold medallist

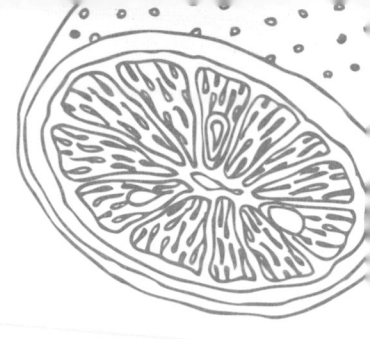

My mother always used to say,
'With patience and perseverance
you could take a donkey from
Kinsale to Jerusalem.'

John Spillane, singer/songwriter

My mother used to say,
'Good manners never cost
you anything.'

Rosemary Shrager, chef

My mum still tells me to
'treat everyone with love,
kindness and respect.'

Lorraine Kelly, TV presenter

My mother used to say,
'Sit down, have a cup of tea,
and don't let it go to your head.'

David Blunkett, MP for Sheffield Brightside
and Hillsborough

My mother used to say,
'Watch your language, because it's
a precision tool; it's a scalpel
not an axe.'

Fergal Tobin, publishing director of Gill & McMillan

My mother, Nancy Power,
would say, 'It's not everyone
that money suits.'

Her mother, Elly Power
would say (after farting),
'That would melt a foot of snow.'

My other granny,
Bridie Dowling, would say,
'That fellow would ate [sic] his
way to Calvary and back.'

Christy Moore, singer/songwriter

My mother always said when
we woke up in the morning:
'Your brother puts on his shoes
and you put on your legs.'

Oscar Pistorius, South African athlete,
who runs with prosthetic limbs and is
known as 'Blade Runner'

My mother always used to say,
'Don't get too big for your boots.'

Sir Alex Ferguson CBE, manager of Manchester United FC

My mother and father always used to say, '"How are you?" is a greeting, not a question.'

Maeve Binchy, author

My mother used to say,
'Never put new shoes on the
table, it's bad luck.'

Laila Morse, actress

My mother used to say,
'If you can't find anything nice to say
about anybody, then don't say anything at all.'
It seemed so lacking in originality at the time,
but over the years I've come to think that it's
not a bad motto. I wish a few more
folk would take it to heart.'

She also used to say,
'Never let it be said that your mother
bred a gibber.' I'd like to think that she
wouldn't have been disappointed
on that count.

Alan Titchmarsh, gardener/broadcaster

My mother always used to say,
'Fix yourself up; you're like the
wreck of the *Hesperus*.'

John Kelly, writer/broadcaster

My mother used to say,
'I'm glad you are growing up in
peace time and will never have
to sit in a cellar, praying that the
Americans get to you before
the Russians do.'

Gisela Stuart, MP for Birmingham and Edgbaston

'Stephen,' she'd say when I was
a kid, 'Do you know how to
give God a good laugh?'
'No Mum,' I'd reply, though of
course I knew the answer, as it was a
regular game between us. 'How?'
'You tell him your plans for the
future.' Then she'd smile wisely.
I didn't really get it when I was
young – but I sure do now...

**Stephen Lloyd, MP for Eastbourne**

My mother used to say,
'It's far easier to get into a handlin'
than out of one.'

I also remember her
regular counsel in childhood,
'You don't want to be a notice-box.'
She later updated this sentiment
when I became a Minister to
'Sanity not vanity.'

Mark Durkan, MP for Foyle/former leader
of the SDLP

My mother always used to say,
'When you know you're beaten,
give in gracefully.'

Lord Jeffrey Archer, author/politician

My mother used to say,
'When you see a magpie in Cornwall,
you must salute it with your right
hand and spit over your left shoulder
to ward off evil... but not when you
are driving,'

*and*

(after a minor accident in her
94th year when she was not
wearing a seat belt) 'There's no
fool as an old fool.'

Lord Paul Tyler

# CLASSIC POEMS FOR
# MOTHERS

COMPILED BY MAX MORRIS

# CLASSIC POEMS FOR MOTHERS

Max Morris

ISBN: 978 1 84953 210 5    Hardback    £9.99

*Mother, dear mother, the years have been long*
*Since I last listened your lullaby song:*
*Sing, then, and unto my soul it shall seem*
*Womanhood's years have been only a dream.*
*Clasped to your heart in a loving embrace,*
*With your light lashes just sweeping my face,*
*Never hereafter to wake or to weep;*
*Rock me to sleep, mother, rock me to sleep!*

**Elizabeth Chase Allen, from 'Rock Me to Sleep'**

Throughout the centuries, poets have been inspired by mothers – their joys and sorrows, their loyalty and love, and the many trials and triumphs they experience as they watch their children grow.

This exquisitely illustrated anthology contains inspiring and moving poetry for mothers by some of the best-loved writers in the English language, from Anne Bradstreet to William Wordsworth, and from Emily Dickinson to Rudyard Kipling.

To share your
own inherited words of
wisdom, email Valerie at
valentinebowe@gmail.com

www.summersdale.com